Student Workbo

MW01680176

Earth Science

Robert H. Marshall
Allen Rosskopf

AGS®
American Guidance Service, Inc.
Circle Pines, Minnesota 55014-1796

Credits

Gary Walchli, Cover Photo

Printed in the United States of America

ISBN 0-88671-951-8 (Previously ISBN 0-7916-0102-1)

Order Number 80232

A 0 9 8 7 6

Contents

ENGLISH SYSTEM MEASUREMENTS

Distance

1 mile	=	1,760 yards
1 mile	=	5,280 feet
1 mile	=	63,360 inches
1 yard	=	3 feet
1 yard	=	36 inches
1 foot	=	12 inches

Weight (mass)

1 ton	=	2,000 pounds
1 ton	=	32,000 ounces
1 pound	=	16 ounces

Volume

1 gallon	=	4 quarts
1 gallon	=	8 pints
1 gallon	=	16 cups
1 quart	=	2 pints
1 quart	=	4 cups
1 pint	=	2 cups

METRIC SYSTEM MEASUREMENTS

Distance

1 kilometer	=	1,000 meters
1 meter	=	100 centimeters
1 meter	=	1,000 millimeters
1 centimeter	=	10 millimeters

Weight (mass)

1 kilogram	=	1,000 grams
1 gram	=	100 centigrams
1 gram	=	1,000 milligrams
1 centigram	=	10 milligrams

Volume

1 kiloliter	=	1,000 liters
1 liter	=	100 centiliters
1 liter	=	1,000 milliliters
1 centiliter	=	10 milliliters

Note: 1 milliliter is the same as 1 cubic centimeter.

METRIC EQUIVALENTS

1 kilometer	=	.6 miles
1 meter	=	1.1 yards
1 meter	=	3.3 feet
1 centimeter	=	.4 inches
1 liter	=	.26 gallons
1 liter	=	1.06 quarts
1 kilogram	=	2.2 pounds
1 gram	=	.035 ounces

1 mile	=	1.6 kilometers
1 yard	=	.9 meters
1 foot	=	.303 meters
1 inch	=	2.54 centimeters
1 gallon	=	3.8 liters
1 quart	=	.95 liters
1 pound	=	.45 kilograms
1 ounce	=	28 grams

CHANGING ENGLISH UNITS OF MEASUREMENT

Directions: When working in science, it is often necessary to change measurements in one unit into another. For example, you might need to change a measurement in inches into the equivalent number of feet. Use the reference sheet on page 5 to complete the following conversions.

Part A. Distance

Example:	5 feet =	? inches	
Solution:	Since 1 foot =	12 inches,	
	5 feet =	5×12	= 60 inches

1. 2 yards = __________ inches
2. 2 miles = __________ feet
3. 5 miles = __________ yards
4. 10 yards = __________ feet
5. 8 feet = __________ inches
6. $1^1/_2$ miles = __________ feet
7. 3.5 feet = __________ inches
8. 2 miles = __________ inches
9. 6 yards = __________ inches
10. 20 feet = __________ inches

Part B. Weight

Example:	2 pounds =	? ounces	
Solution:	Since 1 pound =	16 ounces,	
	2 pounds =	2×16	= 32 ounces

11. 2 tons = __________ pounds
12. 2 tons = __________ ounces
13. 3.5 tons = __________ pounds
14. 6.5 pounds = __________ ounces

Part C. Volume

Example:	2 gallons =	? quarts	
Solution:	Since 1 gallon =	4 quarts,	
	2 gallons =	2×4	= 8 quarts

15. 3 quarts = __________ cups
16. 2 gallons = __________ cups
17. 4 quarts = __________ cups
18. 3.5 pints = __________ cups
19. 5 quarts = __________ pints
20. 10 pints = __________ cups

CHANGING METRIC UNITS OF MEASUREMENT

Directions: Scientists usually use a measurement system known as the metric system in their experiments. This is because the metric system is easy to work with. All of the units in the metric system are related to each other since they are based on the number 10. Use the reference sheet on page 5 to complete these problems.

Part A. Distance

Example:	5 centimeters	=	? millimeters
Solution:	Since 1 centimeter	=	10 millimeters,
	5 centimeters	=	$5 \times 10 =$ 50 meters

Note these abbreviations:

millimeters = mm	milligrams = mg	milliliters = mL
centimeters = cm	centigrams = cg	centiliters = cL
meters = m	grams = g	liters = L
kilometers = km	kilograms = kg	kiloliters = kL

1.	3 m	=	________	cm	4.	2 km	=	________	m
2.	2 cm	=	________	mm	5.	3.5 cm	=	________	mm
3.	3 m	=	________	mm	6.	9.8 cm	=	________	mm

Part B. Weight

Example:	2 kg	=	? g
Solution:	Since 1 kg	=	1000 g,
	2 kg	=	$2 \times 1000 = 2000$ g

7.	3 cg	=	________	mg	9.	5.9 g	=	________	mg
8.	4 kg	=	________	g	10.	5.2 cg	=	________	mg

Part C. Volume

Example:	2 liters	=	? mL
Solution:	Since 1 liter	=	1000 mL,
	2 liters	=	$2 \times 1000 = 2000$ mL

11.	3 L	=	________	mL	14.	2 cL	=	________	mL
12.	5 L	=	________	mL	15.	4.2 kL	=	________	L
13.	8 L	=	________	cL	16.	5.6 kL	=	________	mL

USING MAP SCALES WITH ENGLISH SYSTEM UNITS

A. *Directions:* Find the actual distance represented by each item. Use a map scale of 1 inch = 4 miles.

Example: 12 inches = 12 × 4 miles = 48 miles

1. 3 inches ______________________
2. 7 inches ______________________
3. 4 inches ______________________
4. 2 inches ______________________
5. 5 inches ______________________
6. 3.5 inches ______________________
7. 2.6 inches ______________________
8. $1^1/_2$ inches ______________________
9. 5.2 inches ______________________
10. $3^1/_2$ inches ______________________

B. *Directions:* Find how many inches on the map would represent each of these actual distances. Use a map scale of 1 inch = 5 miles.

Example: 50 miles = 50 ÷ 5 = 10 inches

11. 10 miles ______________________
12. 15 miles ______________________
13. 25 miles ______________________
14. 20 miles ______________________
15. 30 miles ______________________
16. 8 miles ______________________
17. 13 miles ______________________
18. 18.2 miles ______________________
19. 22.1 miles ______________________
20. 12.3 miles ______________________

C. *Directions:* Find the actual distance in feet represented by each item. Use a map scale of 1 : 5,000.

Example: 3 inches = 3 × 5,000 = 15,000 inches
15,000 inches = 15,000 ÷ 12 = 1,250 feet

21. 2 inches ______________________
22. 4 inches ______________________
23. 3 inches ______________________
24. 5 inches ______________________
25. 7 inches ______________________
26. 3.5 inches ______________________
27. 7.2 inches ______________________
28. 6.8 inches ______________________
29. 4.6 inches ______________________
30. 10 inches ______________________

USING MAP SCALES WITH METRIC SYSTEM UNITS

A. ***Directions:*** Find the actual distance represented by each item. Use a map scale of 1 centimeter = 3 kilometers.

Example: 13 centimeters $= 13 \times 3 = 39$ kilometers

1. 4 centimeters ____________
2. 2 centimeters ____________
3. 8 centimeters ____________
4. 3 centimeters ____________
5. 5 centimeters ____________
6. 8.3 centimeters ____________
7. 11.3 centimeters ____________
8. 12.3 centimeters ____________
9. 4.2 centimeters ____________
10. 5.8 centimeters ____________

B. ***Directions:*** Find how many centimeters on the map would represent each of these actual distances. Use a map scale of 1 centimeter = 4 kilometers.

Example: 40 kilometers $= 40 \div 4 = 10$ centimeters

11. 8 kilometers ____________
12. 16 kilometers ____________
13. 24 kilometers ____________
14. 28 kilometers ____________
15. 32 kilometers ____________
16. 60 kilometers ____________
17. 12 kilometers ____________
18. 10 kilometers ____________
19. 20 kilometers ____________
20. 100 kilometers ____________

C. ***Directions:*** Find the actual distance in meters represented by each item. Use a map scale of 1 : 5,000.

Example: 6 centimeters $= 6 \times 5{,}000 = 30{,}000$ centimeters
30,000 centimeters $= 30{,}000 \div 100 = 300$ meters

21. 3 centimeters ____________
22. 4 centimeters ____________
23. 8 centimeters ____________
24. 2 centimeters ____________
25. 7.2 centimeters ____________
26. 1.8 centimeters ____________
27. 9 centimeters ____________
28. 6.2 centimeters ____________
29. 3.4 centimeters ____________
30. 1.3 centimeters ____________

FORMING SENTENCES

Directions: Unscramble the following words or groups of words to form complete sentences that state main ideas of the chapter.

1. round map   A globe   the earth   is a   of

2. of the   continents   The   called   earth are   solid surfaces

3. of   continents   separate most   Oceans   the major

4. poles are located   earth   The North   bottom   and South   of the   at the   top and

5. rotates   The   axis   on   earth   its

6. east to   the earth   Lines   west around   of latitude run

7. earth into   equator divides   The   the   two hemispheres

8. an   Hemisphere   The Tropic   the Northern   in   of Cancer is   imaginary line

9. map grid   Horizontal   and   a   lines form   vertical

10. once every   hours   The   twenty-four   rotates   earth

FINDING PERCENT

Directions: The table below shows the size and position of the different continents. Complete the table. You are to find the percent of earth's population that lives on each continent. The first continent, Asia, has been done. Use this formula to compute the percents:

Continent's Population	÷	Total Population	=	Continent's Percent of Population

Example: Asia

2,800 million ÷ 4,605 million = .5951115 ≈ 60%

Round to the nearest whole percent.

Continents of the Earth				
Continent	Area (sq. mi.)	Percent of Earth's Area	Population	% of Earth's Population
Asia	17,000,000	29.7	2,800 million	60
Africa	11,700,000	20.4	530 million	
North America	9,400,000	16.3	400 million	
South America	6,900,000	12.0	260 million	
Antarctica	5,100,000	8.0		
Europe	4,000,000	7.0	700 million	
Australia	3,000,000	5.2	15 million	
TOTALS	57,100,000 (sq. mi.)	98.6* (* excludes islands)	4,704 million	

Directions: Complete the circle graph. Draw sections to show the population of each continent.

Percent of Earth's Population on Each Continent

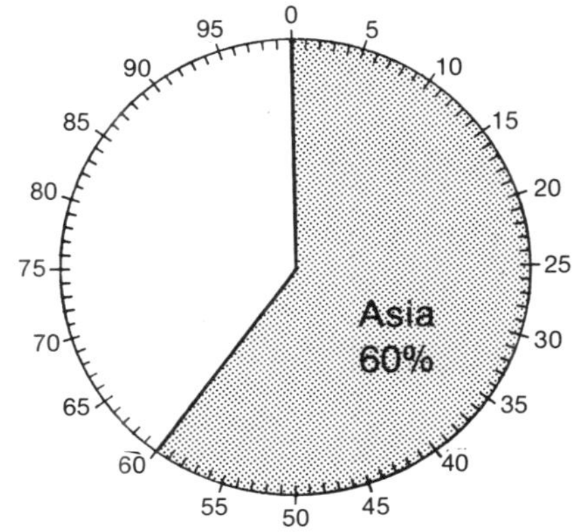

ALIKE AND DIFFERENT

Directions: When you tell how things are alike, you are comparing them. When you tell how they are different, you are contrasting them. Tell how each pair listed below is alike and how it is different.

1. EQUATOR — PRIME MERIDIAN
   a. How they are alike:

   ____

   b. How they are different:

   ____

2. LONGITUDE — LATITUDE
   a. How they are alike:

   ____

   b. How they are different:

   ____

3. NORTH POLE — SOUTH POLE
   a. How they are alike:

   ____

   b. How they are different:

   ____

4. MAP — GLOBE
   a. How they are alike:

   ____

   b. How they are different:

   ____

5. BLOCK GRID — LINE GRID
   a. How they are alike:

   ____

   b. How they are different:

   ____

THE GLOBE

Directions: Suppose you have been asked to explain to a class the major lines on the globe. Use the illustrations below as a guide. Write what you will tell the class on the lines below.

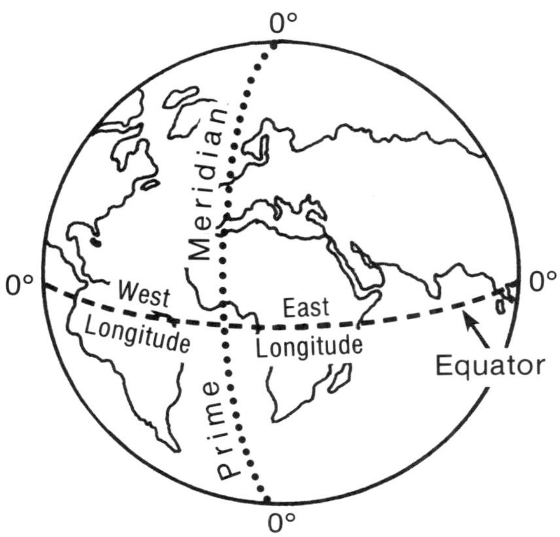

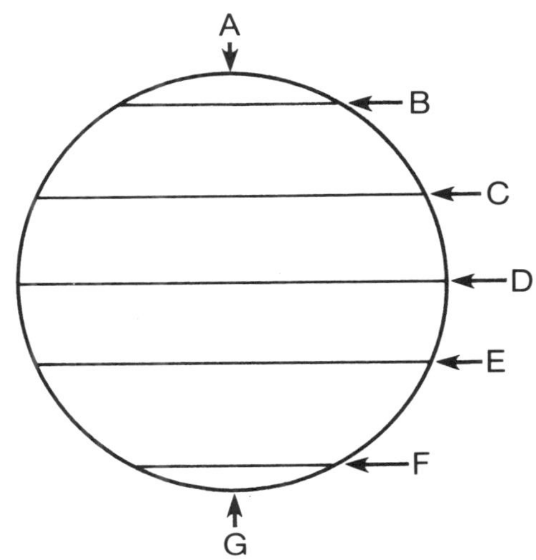

FORMING SENTENCES

Directions: Unscramble the following words or groups of words to form complete sentences that state main ideas of the chapter.

1. path satellite travels planet A around a in a

2. the The natural satellite moon earth's is

3. days to the earth It around complete takes the one revolution moon twenty-nine

4. causes two objects other Gravity each that is to attract the force

5. cause a crater When an it may object hits the moon

6. around the its orbit The path be called earth can of the moon

7. ellipse like the of the is an The shape moon's orbit earth's

8. which we as moon The different phases are known ways in see the moon

9. the moon the earth the sun When and a solar eclipse comes between occurs

10. the moon In a lunar over its surface eclipse the earth because creates a shadow becomes darker

ALIKE AND DIFFERENT

Directions: When you tell how things are alike, you are comparing them. When you tell how they are different, you are contrasting them. Tell how each pair listed below is alike and how it is different.

1. REVOLUTION — ROTATION
   a. How they are alike:
   ____
   b. How they are different:
   ____

2. EARTH — MOON
   a. How they are alike:
   ____
   b. How they are different:
   ____

3. CIRCUMFERENCE — DIAMETER
   a. How they are alike:
   ____
   b. How they are different:
   ____

4. LUNAR ECLIPSE — SOLAR ECLIPSE
   a. How they are alike:
   ____
   b. How they are different:
   ____

5. NEW MOON — FULL MOON
   a. How they are alike:
   ____
   b. How they are different:
   ____

THE EARTH AND MOON IN MOTION

Directions: Suppose you have been asked to explain to a class the motions of the earth and moon around the sun. Use the illustration below as a guide. Write what you will tell the class on the lines below.

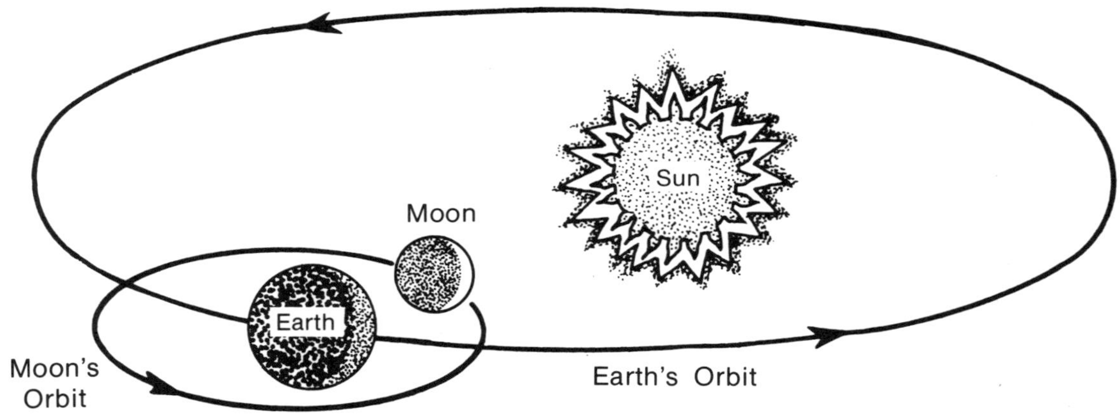

The earth and moon revolve around the sun.

EARTH'S SEASONS

Directions: Suppose you have been asked to explain to a class the seasons of the year. Use the illustration below as a guide. Write what you will tell the class on the lines below.

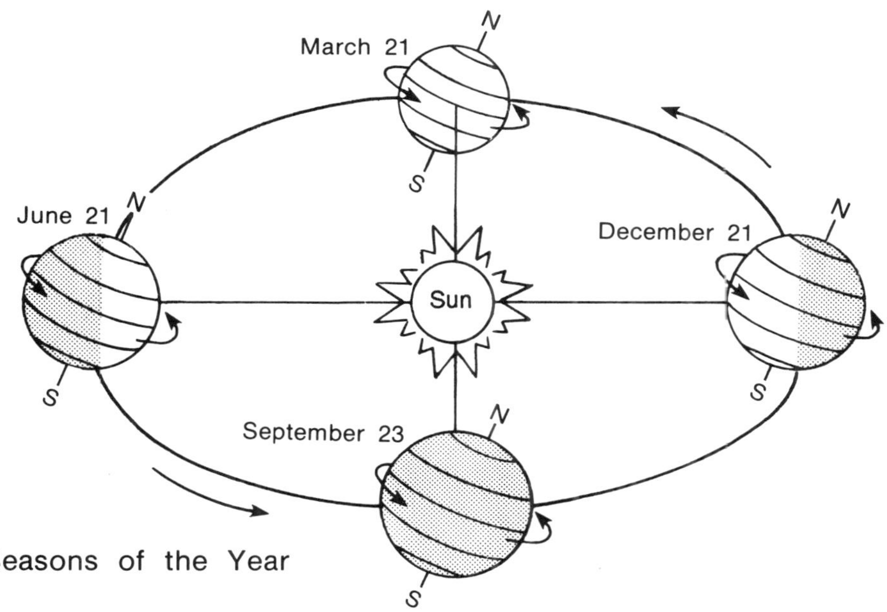

Seasons of the Year

THE PHASES OF THE MOON

Directions: **Suppose you have been asked to explain to a class the phases of the moon. Use the illustrations below as a guide. Write what you will tell the class on the lines below.**

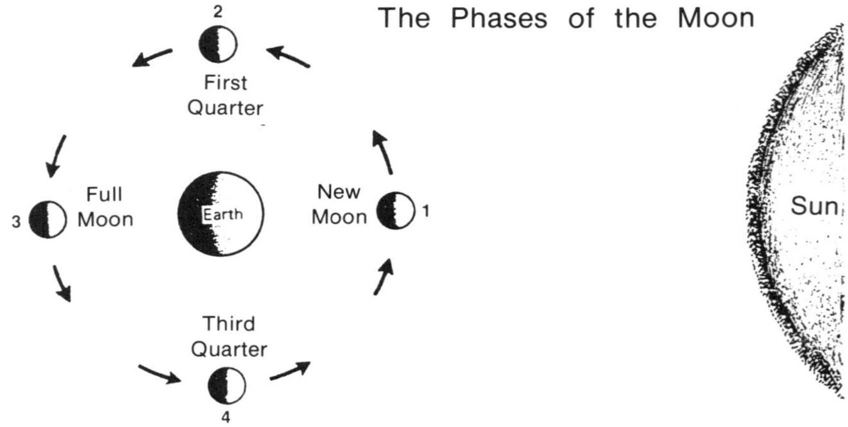

1. New Moon

2. First Quarter

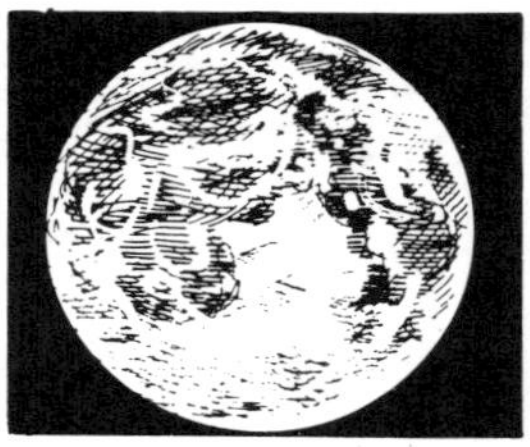

3. Full Moon

4. Third Quarter

EARTH AND MOON CROSSWORD PUZZLE

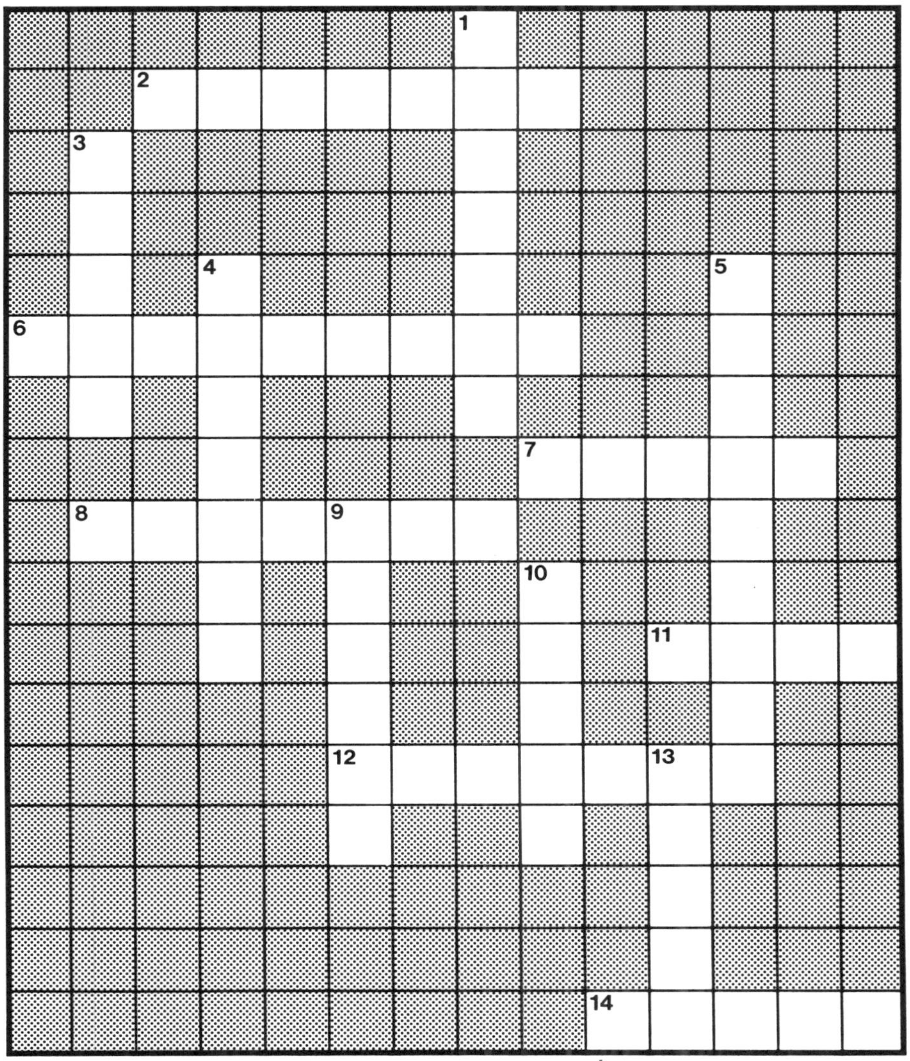

Across

2. Caused by objects hitting the surface of the moon
6. An object that revolves around a celestial body
7. The regular rising and falling of the major bodies of earth's water
8. The oval shape of the earth's orbit
11. The earth's natural satellite
12. The shadow of one heavenly body on another
14. The path a satellite follows as it revolves

Down

1. The force of attraction between all objects in the universe
3. A ____ eclipse occurs when the earth casts a shadow on the moon.
4. Move in curved path around something
5. Makes stars look brighter and bigger than with the naked eye
9. The changes in the way that the moon appears as it orbits earth
10. Flat, low plains on the moon
13. A ____ eclipse occurs when the moon casts a shadow on the earth.

ECLIPSES

Directions: Suppose you have been asked to explain to a class the solar and lunar eclipses. Use the illustrations below as a guide. Write what you will tell the class on the lines below.

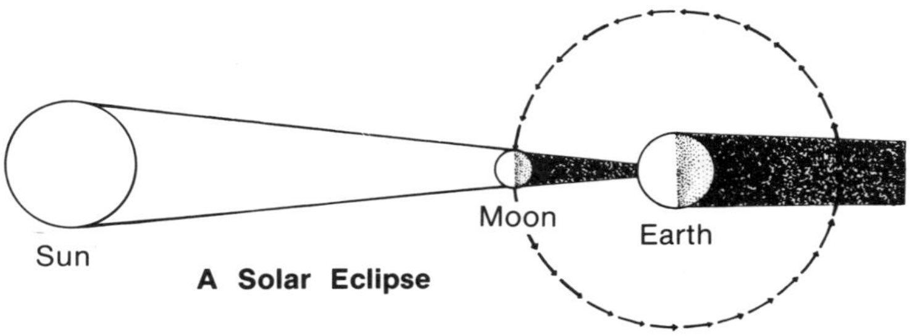

A Solar Eclipse

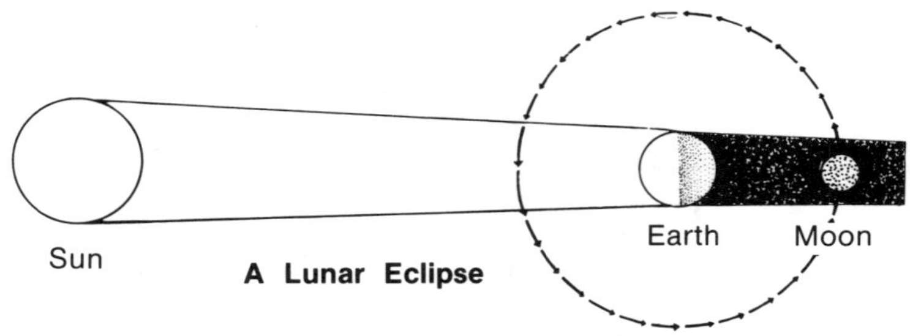

A Lunar Eclipse

VIEWING A SOLAR ECLIPSE

Directions: Suppose you have been asked to explain to a class the proper method of viewing solar eclipses. Use the illustration below as a guide. Write what you will tell the class on the lines below.

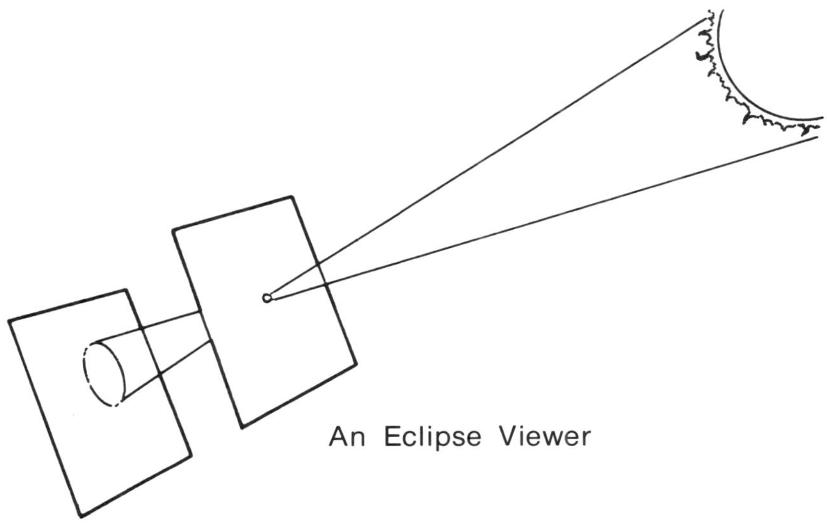

An Eclipse Viewer

ALIKE AND DIFFERENT

Directions: When you tell how things are alike, you are comparing them. When you tell how they are different, you are contrasting them. Tell how each pair listed below is alike and how it is different.

1. STAR — PLANET
   a. How they are alike:

   ____

   b. How they are different:

   ____

2. INNER PLANETS — OUTER PLANETS
   a. How they are alike:

   ____

   b. How they are different:

   ____

3. COMET — ASTEROID
   a. How they are alike:

   ____

   b. How they are different:

   ____

4. MERCURY — PLUTO
   a. How they are alike:

   ____

   b. How they are different:

   ____

5. SATURN — JUPITER
   a. How they are alike:

   ____

   b. How they are different:

   ____

SOLAR SYSTEM CROSSWORD PUZZLE

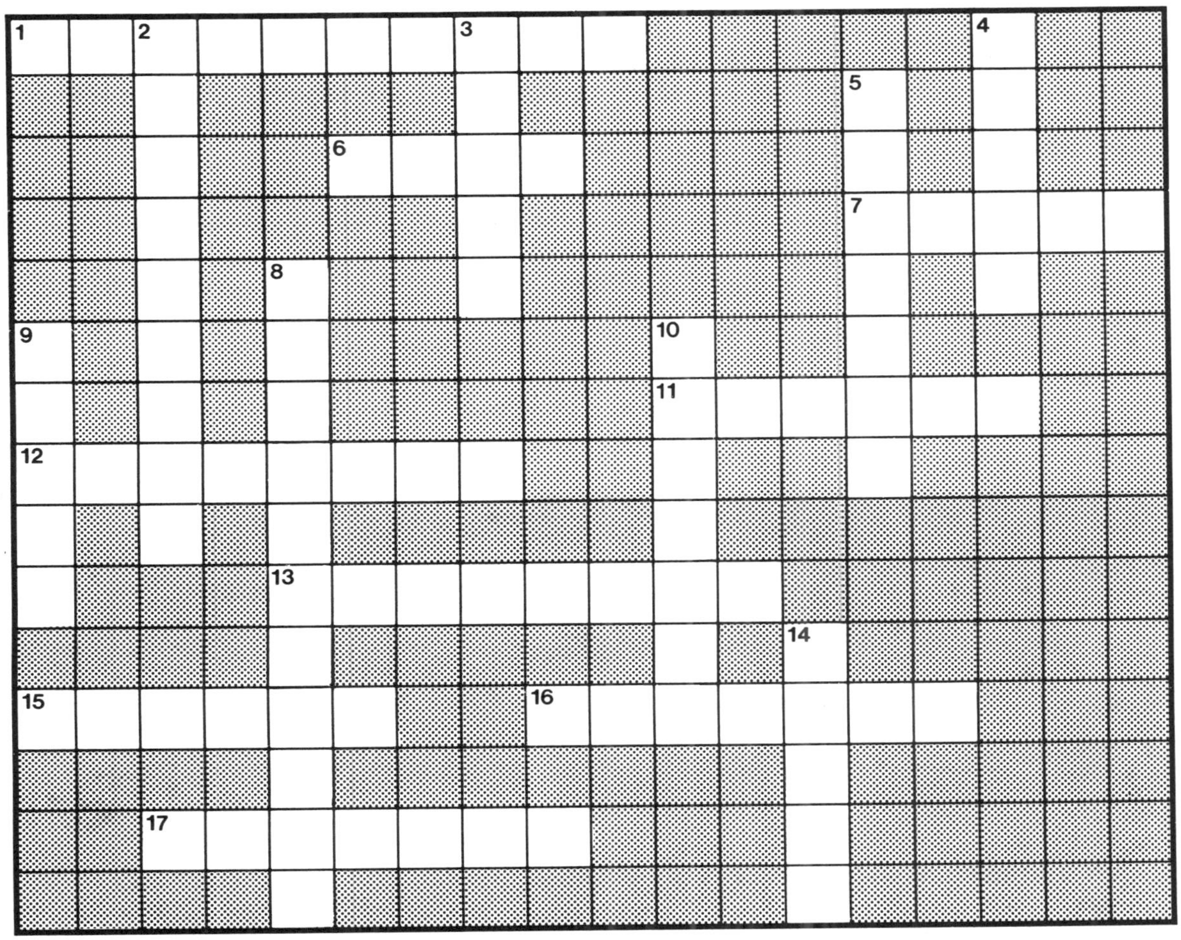

Across

1. An envelope of gas surrounding a celestial body
6. The red planet; named for the Roman god of war
7. Considered the outermost planet
11. Planet with a tilted axis; appears to be on its side
12. A body, smaller than a planet, that orbits a star
13. Cooler areas on the surface of the sun that appear darker
15. The planet known for its rings
16. Fastest-moving planet
17. Satellites of stars

Down

2. Part of an asteroid that hits the earth
3. Planet third from the sun
4. Planet that rotates in the opposite direction from the others
5. Green planet; cannot be seen without a telescope
8. The inner planets; most like earth
9. Objects in the sky that generate light
10. The largest planet
14. Five planets; made mostly of gases

THE MATHEMATICAL CONSTANT, π

In mathematics, the symbol π stands for the number 3.14. π is found by dividing the circumference of a circle by its diameter. Read the following definitions.

Circumference — the distance around a circle.
Diameter — the length of a straight line drawn through the center of a circle.

Now, look at the following diagram. The diameter of the circle is two inches. The circumference is 6.28 inches.

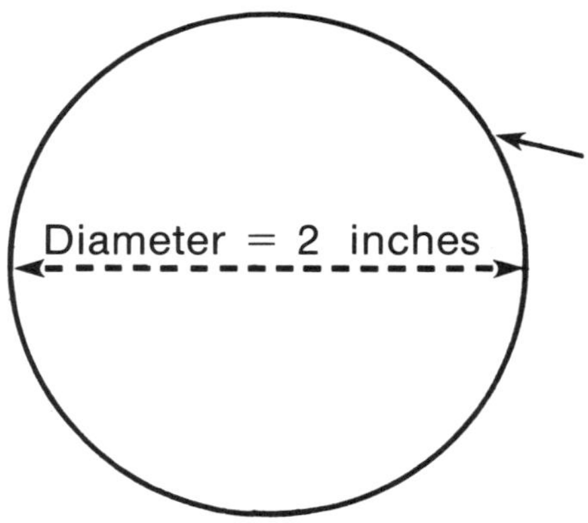

Circumference = 6.28 inches

Circumference	÷	Diameter	=	π
6.28	÷	2	=	3.14

A circumference of 6.28 inches divided by the diameter of 2 inches equals 3.14, which is π. No matter what circle you draw, the circumference divided by the diameter is equal to 3.14.

Directions: Measure the diameter of each of these circles. Then calculate the circumference.

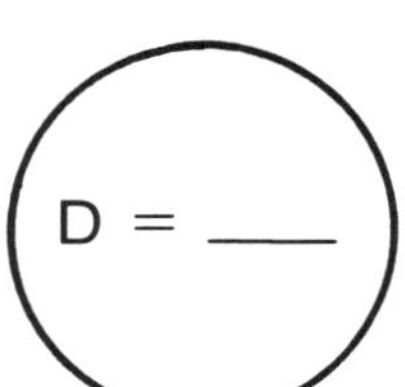

1. ________

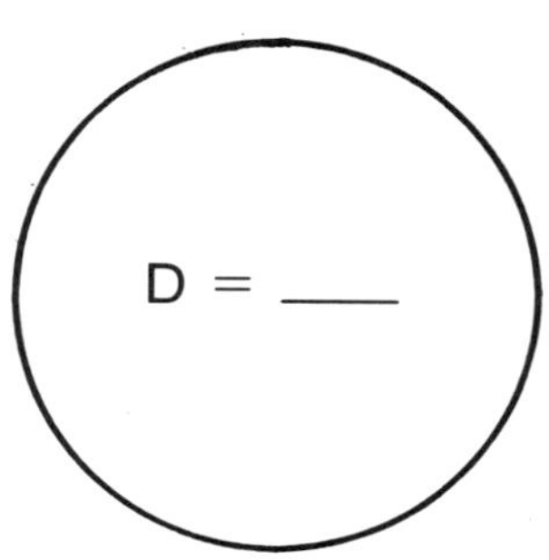

2. ________

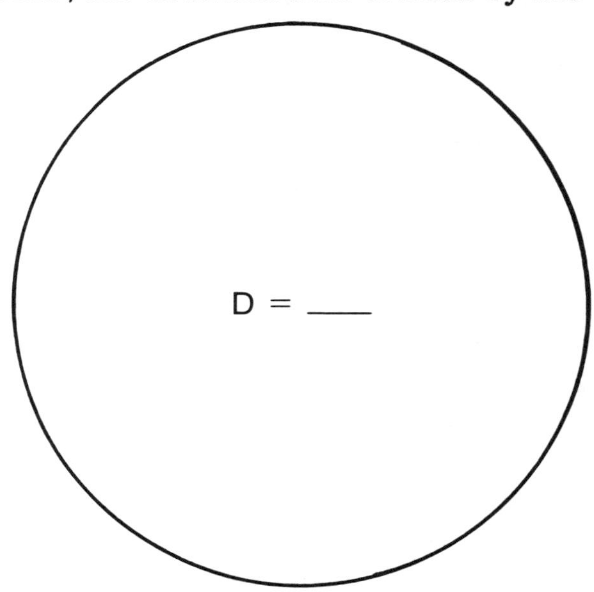

3. ________

FINDING THE CIRCUMFERENCE

Astronomers use π to calculate the circumference of a planet or star.
Since π = circumference ÷ diameter:

Circumference = π times diameter
The diameter of the earth is 7,900 miles.

What is earth's circumference?

Circumference = π times diameter

Circumference = 3.14 times 7,900

Circumference = 24,806 miles

Directions: Find the circumference for each object below. Write the answer in the circumference column in the chart.

Solar System Circumferences		
Object	**Diameter (miles)**	**Circumference**
Sun	865,000	
Mercury	3,000	
Venus	7,700	
Earth	7,900	*24,806 miles*
Moon	2,160	
Mars	4,200	
Jupiter	88,730	
Saturn	75,060	
Uranus	29,600	
Neptune	27,700	
Pluto	unknown	*unknown*

CLASSIFICATION: THE SOLAR SYSTEM

Directions: Identify each part of the solar system in the diagram below. Write the answer on each line. Then place each planet in the categories to which it belongs. Planets will often be used in more than one category. The number of lines shown may be more than you need.

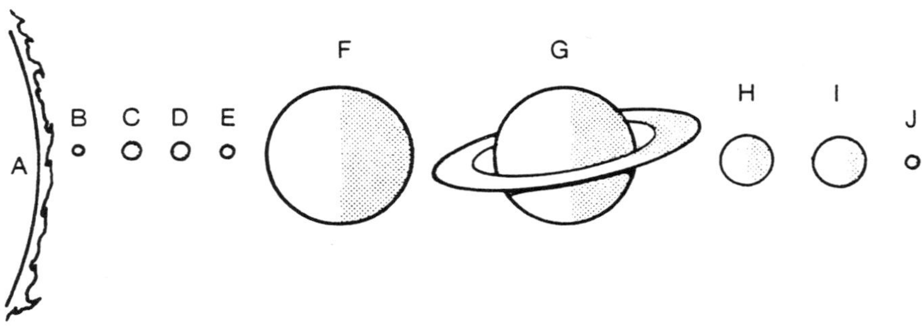

A. ____________________

B. ____________________

C. ____________________

D. ____________________

E. ____________________

F. ____________________

G. ____________________

H. ____________________

I. ____________________

J. ____________________

1. Inner Planets	2. Outer Planets	3. Planets Without Satellites
______	______	______
______	______	______
______	______	______
______	______	______
______	______	______

4. Terrestrial Planets	5. Planets with Two or More Satellites	6. Planets with Five or More Satellites
______	______	______
______	______	______
______	______	______
______	______	______
______	______	______

FORMING SENTENCES

Directions: Unscramble the following words or groups of words to form complete sentences that state main ideas of the chapter.

1. related to color a star its The temperature of is

   ____

2. are of kinds There magnitude two

   ____

3. are in we can All of constellations that see our own the galaxy

   ____

   ____

4. explodes called A star a is supernova that

   ____

5. stars called are supergiants The largest

   ____

6. nearest over miles The away trillion star twenty-five is

   ____

   ____

7. is see in the sky that you pattern a star A constellation can

   ____

   ____

8. end Most their at of collapse stars the lives

   ____

9. distance in the light-years We to measure stars

   ____

10. energy Dwarf off little stars give very

    ____

ALIKE AND DIFFERENT

Directions: When you tell how things are alike, you are comparing them. When you tell how they are different, you are contrasting them. Tell how each pair listed below is alike and how it is different.

1. SUPERGIANT — DWARF
   a. How they are alike:

   ____

   b. How they are different:

   ____

2. LIGHT-YEAR — MILE
   a. How they are alike:

   ____

   b. How they are different:

   ____

3. SPIRAL — ELLIPTICAL
   a. How they are alike:

   ____

   b. How they are different:

   ____

4. BLUE-WHITE — RED
   a. How they are alike:

   ____

   b. How they are different:

   ____

5. ABSOLUTE MAGNITUDE — APPARENT MAGNITUDE
   a. How they are alike:

   ____

   b. How they are different:

   ____

WRITING LARGE NUMBERS

Many of the measurements that deal with the planets and stars are very large. Study the following chart. Then complete the problems.

Number	Number in Words
1,000	one thousand
1,000,000	one million
1,000,000,000	one billion
1,000,000,000,000	one trillion

A. *Directions:* Write the underlined numbers in words.

1. The diameter of Jupiter = 88,730 miles.

 ____

2. The distance of Jupiter from the sun = 483,000,000 miles.

 ____

3. The distance of Earth from the sun = 93,000,000 miles.

 ____

4. The distance of Uranus from the sun = 1,782,000,000 miles.

 ____

5. The diameter of Neptune = 27,700 miles.

 ____

B. *Directions:* Write these sentences, but use numbers instead of number words.

6. The speed of light is one hundred eighty six thousand miles per second.

 ____

7. One light-year is equal to five trillion, eight hundred sixty five billion, six hundred ninety million miles.

 ____

8. The temperature of a red star is five thousand, five hundred degrees.

 ____

9. The distance of the moon from earth is two hundred forty thousand miles.

 ____

10. The diameter of the sun is eight hundred sixty five thousand miles.

 ____

EARTH CHEMISTRY CROSSWORD PUZZLE

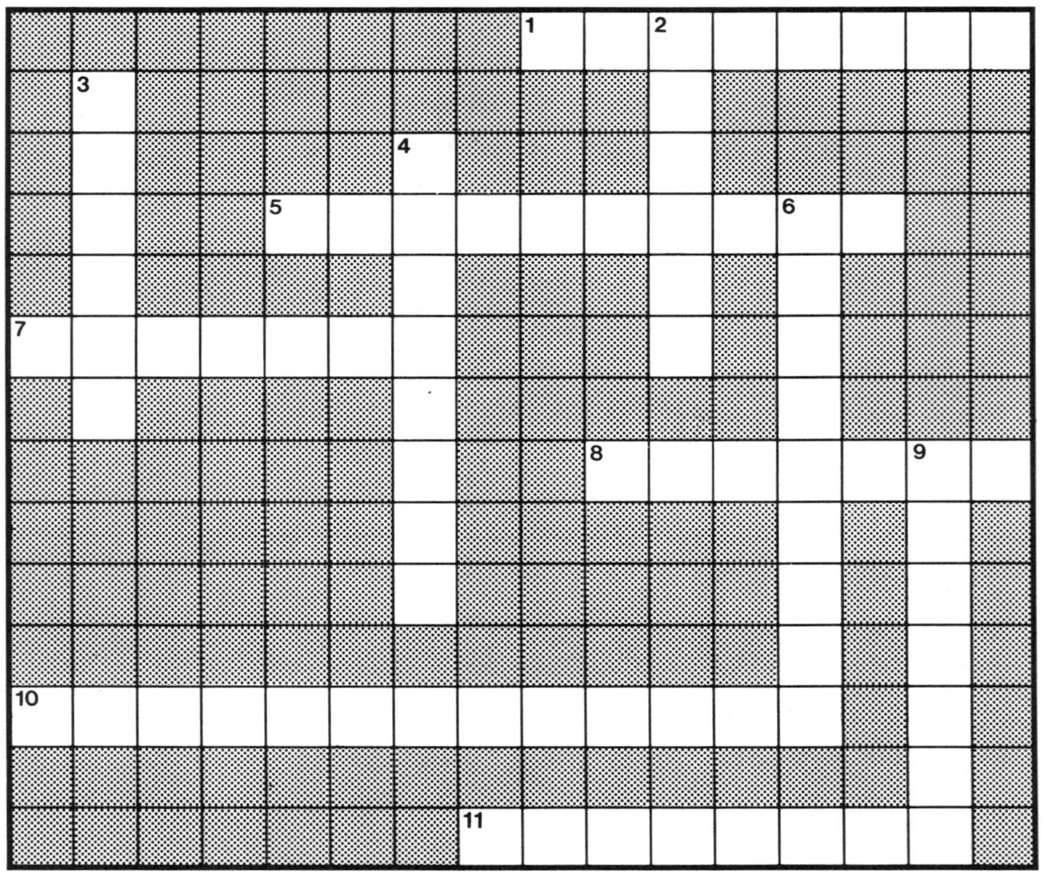

Across

1. Matter that is formed from two or more different elements
5. Characteristics that help you to identify matter
7. Two or more elements or compounds that are simply mixed together
8. The number of electrons is equal to the number of _____ .
10. NaCl and Fe_2O_3 are scientific _____ .
11. Gold, iron, oxygen, and lead are all _____ .

Down

2. Anything that has weight and takes up space
3. Three states of matter: solid, ______ , and gas
4. The smallest unit of a compound
6. The number of _____ is equal to the number of protons.
9. The center of the atom

ALIKE AND DIFFERENT

Directions: When you tell how things are alike, you are comparing them. When you tell how they are different, you are contrasting them. Tell how each pair listed below is alike and how it is different.

1. ELEMENT — COMPOUND
   a. How they are alike:

   ____

   b. How they are different:

   ____

2. SOLID — GAS
   a. How they are alike:

   ____

   b. How they are different:

   ____

3. PROTON — ELECTRON
   a. How they are alike:

   ____

   b. How they are different:

   ____

4. MIXTURE — COMPOUND
   a. How they are alike:

   ____

   b. How they are different:

   ____

5. EVAPORATION — CONDENSATION
   a. How they are alike:

   ____

   b. How they are different:

   ____

MINERAL MINING WORD SEARCH

Directions: There are 15 minerals hidden in this puzzle. The words go across and down. First find each mineral in the puzzle. Then choose from the words you find to write the name of the correct mineral next to the common use listed below.

B	A	U	X	I	T	E	B	C	F	H	D	N	N	R
P	Y	R	I	T	E	J	K	D	L	Y	Y	I	I	H
G	U	A	Q	G	O	L	D	O	U	C	W	D	F	A
S	L	L	V	E	R	L	U	T	O	O	B	Y	C	L
B	O	H	S	F	S	L	Q	G	R	P	G	M	O	I
F	E	L	D	S	P	A	R	R	I	P	A	O	R	T
J	D	G	A	D	W	V	T	A	T	E	R	U	U	E
C	A	L	C	I	T	E	A	P	E	R	N	A	N	Q
G	X	J	D	A	N	U	L	H	L	I	E	R	D	S
E	O	M	G	M	M	G	C	I	G	B	T	T	U	W
P	G	C	X	O	W	X	B	T	A	Q	Z	Z	N	D
W	C	D	W	N	P	A	G	E	F	P	V	Z	O	G
W	Y	J	M	D	R	J	M	D	G	J	A	Y	F	Q
J	M	O	C	W	E	D	O	B	I	F	G	T	B	K
K	Q	G	M	Y	L	U	C	N	A	U	J	S	A	U

1. Used in making red sandpaper. ______________________
2. Clear crystal in an engagement ring. ______________________
3. Ground into bath powder. ______________________
4. Found in table salt. ______________________
5. Yellow mineral used in computer chips. ______________________
6. Commonly found in coins and tooth fillings. ______________________
7. Clear crystal used in watches. ______________________
8. Mineral that dissolves to form caves. ______________________
9. Known as "fool's gold." ______________________
10. The "lead" in a pencil. ______________________

ALIKE AND DIFFERENT

Directions: When you tell how things are alike, you are comparing them. When you tell how they are different, you are contrasting them. Tell how each pair listed below is alike and how it is different.

1. CLEAVAGE — FRACTURE
   a. How they are alike:

   ____

   b. How they are different:

   ____

2. MOHS SCALE — FIELD SCALE
   a. How they are alike:

   ____

   b. How they are different:

   ____

3. COLOR — LUSTER
   a. How they are alike:

   ____

   b. How they are different:

   ____

4. SPECIFIC GRAVITY — WEIGHT
   a. How they are alike:

   ____

   b. How they are different:

   ____

5. CALCITE — FLUORITE
   a. How they are alike:

   ____

   b. How they are different:

   ____

THE MOST IMPORTANT THING ABOUT . . .

(This research writing activity may be done individually or in groups.)

Directions: Choose one area of earth science from the box.

Mapping the Earth	Mapping	The Earth and Moon System
Stars and Galaxies	Minerals	The Solar System
Earth Chemistry		

List as many topics as you can think of about the area you selected. Use your textbook as a reference. For example, if you chose "The Solar System," the topics could be: planets, orbits, the sun, the inner planets, the outer planets, comets, space travel, asteroids, and so forth. Record your area and topics in the following spaces:

My Area Is: ________________________________

Possible Topics: ________________________________

____

____

____

____

____

Look at your list of possible topics and choose the one that you feel is the most interesting. Record the topic you chose.

My Topic Is: ________________________________

Use your textbook. Write down all the significant details you can find about the topic you chose. You may also use any other references that you find. After writing the details down, number them in order of decreasing importance. For example, if you had chosen "The Sun" as your topic, you could write down the following:

Importance	**Details**
2	The sun is at the center of the solar system.
1	The sun gives heat and light to the planets.
5	The sun's mass is 99% of the solar system.
3	Light is given off by the photosphere.
4	The sun is a yellow star.
6	The sun is 93,000,000 miles from the earth.

THE MOST IMPORTANT THING ABOUT . . . (Part 2)

Record your details and their importance in the spaces provided.

Importance	Details
______________________	____
______________________	____
______________________	____
______________________	____
______________________	____
______________________	____
______________________	____
______________________	____

Now, write your significant details in the form shown below. You will emphasize the most important thing on your list by writing it in this form.

> The most important thing about the sun is that it gives heat and light to the planets.
>
> The sun is at the center of the solar system.
>
> Light is given off by the photosphere.
>
> The sun is a yellow star.
>
> The sun's mass is 99% of the solar system.
>
> The sun is 93,000,000 miles from the earth.
>
> But, the most important thing about the sun is that it gives heat and light to the planets.

The most important thing about ____

____

____

____

____

____

____

But, the most important thing about ____________________________________

____

____

THE MOST IMPORTANT THING ABOUT . . . (Part 3)

Now, rewrite each of your statements to say the same thing in another way. The example using the sun is rewritten here to demonstrate.

> The most important thing about the sun is that it supplies energy to the entire solar system.
> The planets revolve around the sun.
> The planets receive light energy from the photosphere.
> The sun is a blazing yellow star.
> The sun is bigger than all the rest of the solar system put together.
> It is 93,000,000 miles from the earth to the sun.
> But, the most important thing about the sun is that it supplies energy to the entire solar system.

Write your sample here:

The most important thing about ________________________________

____

____

____

____

____

____

But, the most important thing about ________________________________

____

____

You are now ready to write your final statement on the topic you chose. Compare your two versions of the most important thing. Choose the best statement for each idea. Write your final version neatly on page 37. The final version for the example is shown below.

> The most important thing about the sun is that it gives heat and light to the planets.
> The planets revolve around the sun.
> Light is given off by the photosphere.
> The sun is a blazing yellow star.
> The sun is bigger than all the rest of the solar system put together.
> The sun is 93,000,000 miles from the earth.
> But, the most important thing about the sun is that it gives heat and light to the planets.

The most important thing about . . .

The most important thing about ______________________________

____

____

____

____

____

____

____

____

____

____

But, the most important thing about ______________________________

____

____

____

____

Author(s): ______________________________

____

FORMING SENTENCES

Directions: Unscramble the following words or groups of words to form complete sentences that state main ideas of the chapter.

1. volcanoes surface earth Magma the through of the reaches

   ____

2. minerals of are Rocks collections

   ____

3. form layers are of particles together rocks when Sedimentary pressed

   ____

   ____

4. cools larger more rock are crystals The the the slowly

   ____

   ____

5. fine-grained rocks Extrusive rocks that cooled rapidly are

   ____

6. rocks rocks are cooled called that Coarse-grained intrusive slowly

   ____

   ____

7. is metamorphic banded rock Schist a

   ____

8. gases many formed holes Pumice small escaping has by

   ____

9. Granite common rock most is the intrusive igneous

   ____

10. A rock that remains of living organisms classified as sedimentary rock a nonclastic forms from the is

    ____

    ____

ROCK PROSPECTING

Directions: Search through the letters below to find important words for the study of rocks. Circle each word that you find.

metamorphic	sedimentary	extrusive	gneiss
intrusive	minerals	obsidian	magma
granite	clastic	volcano	lava
igneous	crust	banded	

M	R	D	S	X	E	B	N	G	W	Y	J	P	B	H	D	F	I	S	H
E	E	T	W	P	S	U	Q	X	W	R	X	Z	K	O	G	B	F	K	W
X	J	W	L	L	S	A	H	O	R	A	F	P	Z	H	X	V	F	A	A
D	R	R	M	K	P	A	M	S	L	T	L	C	J	O	X	G	M	Q	E
N	P	J	L	B	L	Q	U	G	A	N	B	Z	L	O	R	I	F	J	B
X	C	O	O	G	T	J	V	O	A	E	D	O	B	A	N	A	D	T	G
X	L	L	L	A	M	A	W	J	B	M	V	S	N	E	S	X	X	V	X
K	E	V	I	S	U	R	T	X	E	L	I	I	R	A	K	T	Z	H	T
C	K	O	O	U	O	L	F	T	V	D	T	A	B	Y	C	G	I	V	J
E	A	S	D	K	D	P	A	H	I	E	L	V	E	A	Z	L	C	C	X
Q	A	F	G	W	K	M	G	A	S	S	R	A	I	G	N	E	O	U	S
G	V	K	N	C	O	G	N	U	U	G	B	L	L	L	O	D	H	V	P
X	L	F	C	R	P	O	E	A	R	Z	H	V	U	Q	K	L	E	F	X
H	X	N	P	A	F	J	I	Z	T	S	U	R	C	X	J	P	V	D	J
C	J	H	L	H	V	O	S	C	N	M	N	E	K	X	Q	I	L	I	P
N	I	K	J	R	P	X	S	R	I	C	V	L	T	H	M	W	N	M	J
C	L	S	M	L	R	S	L	G	E	L	A	V	O	Y	Z	A	N	K	S

Directions: Use each of the words you have found to fill in the blanks in the following sentences. The first letter of each missing word is given.

1. O ______________ is an i ______________ rock of the e ______________ type because it is formed from l ___________ , which flows out of a v ____________ .
2. I ________________________ rocks are a type of igneous rock, which is formed from m ____________________ inside the c ______________________ of the earth.
3. G ________________ is a b ____________________ m ____________________ rock.
4. The mixture of m _____________ can easily be seen in a piece of g ____________ .
5. C ___________________ is a type of s ____________________________ rock.

FORMATION OF SEDIMENTARY ROCK

Directions: Suppose you have been asked to explain to a class how sedimentary rock is formed. Use the illustration below as a guide. Write what you will tell the class on the lines below.

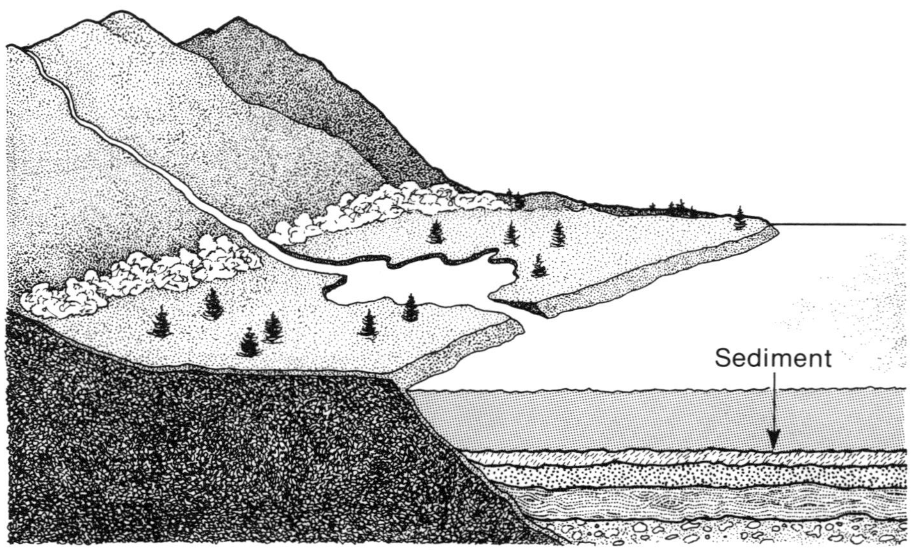

ALIKE AND DIFFERENT

Directions: When you tell how things are alike, you are comparing them. When you tell how they are different, you are contrasting them. Tell how each pair listed below is alike and how it is different.

1. NITROGEN CYCLE — OXYGEN CYCLE
   a. How they are alike:
   ____
   b. How they are different:
   ____

2. IONOSPHERE — TROPOSPHERE
   a. How they are alike:
   ____
   b. How they are different:
   ____

3. RAIN — HAIL
   a. How they are alike:
   ____
   b. How they are different:
   ____

4. CIRRUS — STRATUS
   a. How they are alike:
   ____
   b. How they are different:
   ____

5. WIND — CURRENT
   a. How they are alike:
   ____
   b. How they are different:
   ____

THE STRUCTURE OF THE ATMOSPHERE

Directions: **Suppose you have been asked to explain to a class the layers of the atmosphere. Use the illustration below as a guide. Write what you will tell the class on the lines below.**

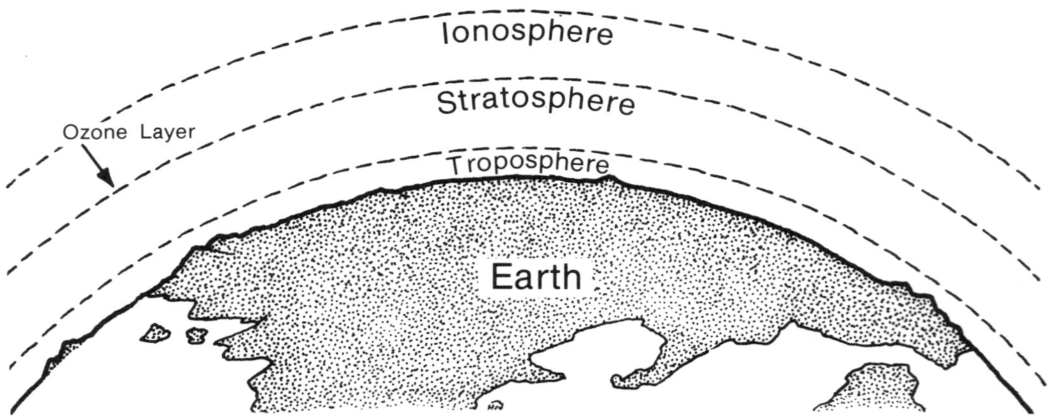

A Model of the Earth's Atmosphere

THE INFLUENCE OF CLOUDS ON THE EARTH

Directions: Suppose you have been asked to explain to a class how clouds affect the temperature of the earth. Use the illustrations below as a guide. Write what you will tell the class on the lines below.

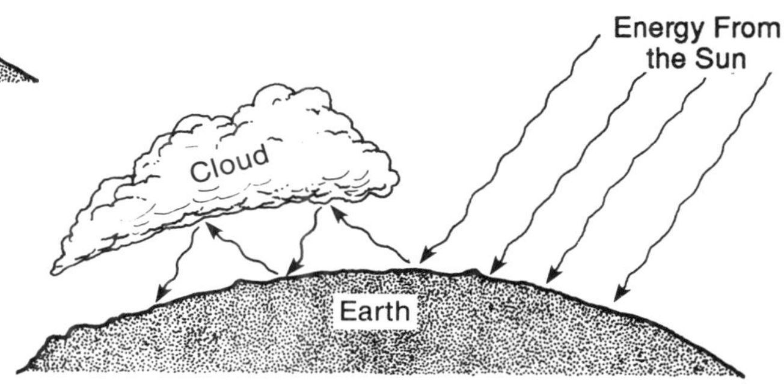

ALIKE AND DIFFERENT

Directions: When you tell how things are alike, you are comparing them. When you tell how they are different, you are contrasting them. Tell how each pair listed below is alike and how it is different.

1. WEATHER — CLIMATE
   a. How they are alike:

      ____

   b. How they are different:

      ____

2. CELSIUS — FAHRENHEIT
   a. How they are alike:

      ____

   b. How they are different:

      ____

3. ANEROID BAROMETER — MERCURY BAROMETER
   a. How they are alike:

      ____

   b. How they are different:

      ____

4. HUMIDITY — RELATIVE HUMIDITY
   a. How they are alike:

      ____

   b. How they are different:

      ____

5. ANEMOMETER — WEATHER VANE
   a. How they are alike:

      ____

   b. How they are different:

      ____

ALIKE AND DIFFERENT

Directions: When you tell how things are alike, you are comparing them. When you tell how they are different, you are contrasting them. Tell how each pair listed below is alike and how it is different.

1. TORNADO — HURRICANE
   a. How they are alike:

   ____

   b. How they are different:

   ____

2. COLD FRONT — WARM FRONT
   a. How they are alike:

   ____

   b. How they are different:

   ____

3. HIGH PRESSURE AREA — LOW PRESSURE AREA
   a. How they are alike:

   ____

   b. How they are different:

   ____

4. POLAR CLIMATE — TROPICAL CLIMATE
   a. How they are alike:

   ____

   b. How they are different:

   ____

5. ICE CAP — TUNDRA
   a. How they are alike:

   ____

   b. How they are different:

   ____

THE CLIMATES OF THE WORLD

Directions: One type of climate in each of the climatic zones is listed below. Read the characteristics for each climate. Then make a travel list of special clothing or supplies you would need if you were going to visit the area and stay outside.

A Visit to the Climate Zones of the World

A. POLAR CLIMATE : Tundra

1. Temperature slightly higher than ice cap
2. Precipitation less than 10 inches per year
3. Soil frozen most of the year
4. Mosses and small shrubs

Special clothing, supplies, and equipment: ______________________

____

____

____

B. TEMPERATE CLIMATE : Humid subtropical

1. Warm and humid summer, mild winter
2. Precipitation 30-65 inches per year
3. Heavy plant growth and forests

Special clothing, supplies, and equipment: ______________________

____

____

____

C. TROPICAL CLIMATE: Tropical rain forest

1. Always hot and humid
2. Precipitation usually over 100 inches per year
3. Very thick forest and plant growth

Special clothing, supplies, and equipment: ______________________

____

____

____

ALIKE AND DIFFERENT

Directions: When you tell how things are alike, you are comparing them. When you tell how they are different, you are contrasting them. Tell how each pair listed below is alike and how it is different.

1. GROUNDWATER — RUNOFF
   a. How they are alike:

   ____

   b. How they are different:

   ____

2. FRESHWATER — SALTWATER
   a. How they are alike:

   ____

   b. How they are different:

   ____

3. RIVER — LAKE
   a. How they are alike:

   ____

   b. How they are different:

   ____

4. GEYSER — HOT SPRING
   a. How they are alike:

   ____

   b. How they are different:

   ____

5. CONTINENTAL SHELF — SHORELINE
   a. How they are alike:

   ____

   b. How they are different:

   ____

ALIKE AND DIFFERENT

Directions: When you tell how things are alike, you are comparing them. When you tell how they are different, you are contrasting them. Tell how each pair listed below are alike and how they are different.

1. MEANDER — OXBOW LAKE
   a. How they are alike:

   ____

   b. How they are different:

   ____

2. EVAPORATION — PRECIPITATION
   a. How they are alike:

   ____

   b. How they are different:

   ____

3. PLANKTON — BENTHOS
   a. How they are alike:

   ____

   b. How they are different:

   ____

4. OCEAN RIDGE — OCEAN TRENCH
   a. How they are alike:

   ____

   b. How they are different:

   ____

5. NEKTON — BENTHOS
   a. How they are alike:

   ____

   b. How they are different:

   ____

CLASSIFYING WORDS AND TERMS

Directions: Read the words and terms in each category below. Choose the two items in each group that do not belong. Cross them out. Write them in their correct categories. Then add two new items of your own to each category.

Rocks
igneous
clastic
hemisphere
intrusive
metamorphic
lithosphere
eclipse

____
____
____
____
____

Maps
globe
Mohs scale
orbit
latitude
meridian
compass
cartographer

____
____
____
____
____

Solar System
rotation
extrusive
planet
revolve
astronomer
satellite
electron

____
____
____
____
____

Chemistry
granite
scientific abbreviation
hydrologist
nucleus
proton
matter
molecule

____
____
____
____
____

Minerals
telescope
cleavage
specific gravity
luster
equator
diamond
quartz

____
____
____
____
____

Water
streak
atom
runoff
geyser
meanders
marine
plankton

____
____
____
____
____

FORMING SENTENCES

Directions: Unscramble the following words or groups of words to form complete sentences that state main ideas of the chapter.

1. breaking into Weathering process is the rock particles of

   ____

2. universal as the is Water solvent known

   ____

3. process carries and to of erosion The locations rocks different soil

   ____

   ____

4. decayed material, fine particles of oxygen, Topsoil has the and greatest amount

   ____

   ____

5. The greatest material water of is mover

   ____

6. Alpine mountain are in glaciers regions found

   ____

7. and rocks sends them sliding or crashing down Gravity breaks loose

   ____

   ____

8. Talus fan-shaped rock fragments mountain areas is a forms in pile of that

   ____

   ____

9. glaciers huge blocks of the A large called is portion held in earth's water of ice

   ____

   ____

10. is a deposit river mouth delta A fan-shaped of a at the

    ____

SORTING WORDS

Directions: Place each of the following words on a line beneath the category to which it belongs. There may be more lines in the category than there are words.

delta	cirque	arete	alluvial fan
sand dune	talus	hanging valley	horn
moraine	mesa	butte	barchan
esker	drumlin	outwash plain	gully
ravine			

Gravity Deposits

____

____

____

____

Wind Deposits

____

____

____

____

Water Deposits

____

____

____

____

Glacier Deposits

____

____

____

____

Eroded Land Forms Caused by Water

____

____

____

____

Eroded Land Forms Caused by Glaciers

____

____

____

____

ALIKE AND DIFFERENT

Directions: When you tell how things are alike, you are comparing them. When you tell how they are different, you are contrasting them. Tell how each pair listed below is alike and how it is different.

1. WEATHERING — EROSION
   a. How they are alike:
   ____
   b. How they are different:
   ____
2. CHEMICAL WEATHERING — MECHANICAL WEATHERING
   a. How they are alike:
   ____
   b. How they are different:
   ____
3. TOPSOIL — SUBSOIL
   a. How they are alike:
   ____
   b. How they are different:
   ____
4. ALPINE GLACIER — CONTINENTAL GLACIER
   a. How they are alike:
   ____
   b. How they are different:
   ____
5. LANDSLIDE — SOIL CREEP
   a. How they are alike:
   ____
   b. How they are different:
   ____

ALIKE AND DIFFERENT

Directions: When you tell how things are alike, you are comparing them. When you tell how they are different, you are contrasting them. Tell how each pair listed below is alike and how it is different.

1. DELTA — TALUS SLOPE
   a. How they are alike:

   ____

   b. How they are different:

   ____

2. GULLIES — STREAMS
   a. How they are alike:

   ____

   b. How they are different:

   ____

3. TILL — STRATIFIED DRIFT
   a. How they are alike:

   ____

   b. How they are different:

   ____

4. MORAINE — DRUMLINS
   a. How they are alike:

   ____

   b. How they are different:

   ____

5. ARETE — CIRQUE
   a. How they are alike:

   ____

   b. How they are different:

   ____

CONTINENTAL DRIFT

Directions: **Suppose you have been asked to explain to a class the theory of continental drift. Use the diagrams below as a guide. Write what you will tell the class on the lines below.**

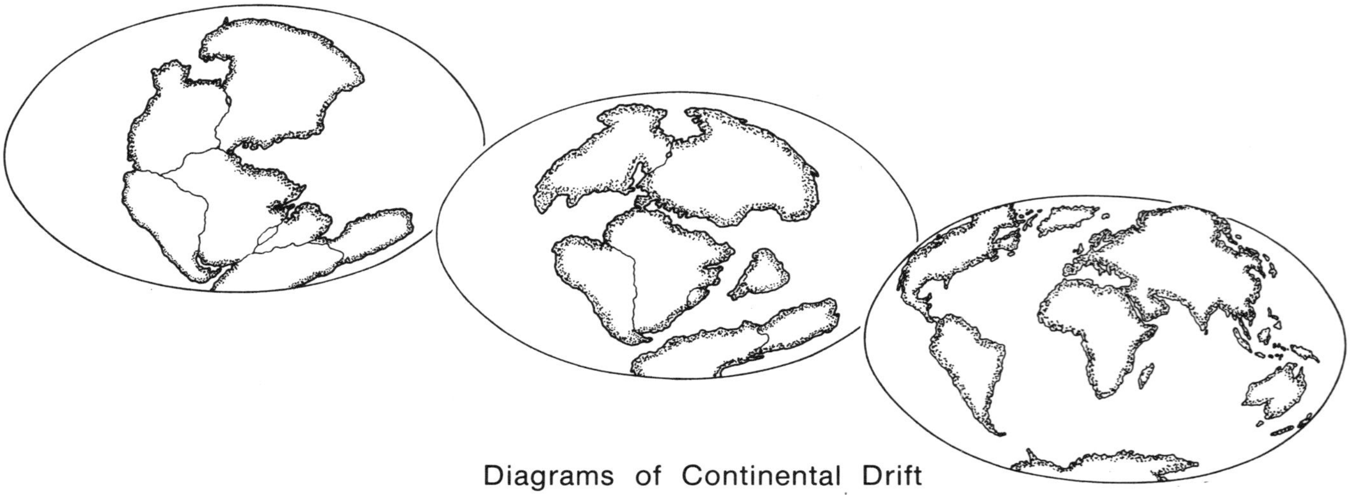

Diagrams of Continental Drift

ALIKE AND DIFFERENT

Directions: When you tell how things are alike, you are comparing them. When you tell how they are different, you are contrasting them. Tell how each pair listed below is alike and how it is different.

1. FRACTURE — FOLD
   a. How they are alike:
   ____
   b. How they are different:
   ____

2. PRIMARY WAVES (P WAVES) — SECONDARY WAVES (S WAVES)
   a. How they are alike:
   ____
   b. How they are different:
   ____

3. CONVECTION THEORY — CONTRACTION THEORY
   a. How they are alike:
   ____
   b. How they are different:
   ____

4. EARTHQUAKE — VOLCANO
   a. How they are alike:
   ____
   b. How they are different:
   ____

5. FOLDED MOUNTAINS — BLOCK FAULT MOUNTAINS
   a. How they are alike:
   ____
   b. How they are different:
   ____

FORMING SENTENCES

Directions: Unscramble the following words or groups of words to form complete sentences that state main ideas of the chapter.

1. and longest is the The earth's history of the Precambrian oldest era

   ____

   ____

2. dinosaurs era of the The Mesozoic is age

   ____

3. Geologic measured units time ranging from is thousands years to billions in of

   ____

   ____

4. relative exact layer of a is not In dating the determined age rock

   ____

   ____

5. pterodactyl reptile that could The was a fly

   ____

6. deposits Coal formed during the Paleozoic were era

   ____

   ____

7. mammals The of age ago began years million seventy

   ____

   ____

8. Absolute in years dating layers is an the rock attempt age of to establish actual

   ____

   ____

9. Jurassic known reptiles the The is of as period age

   ____

   ____

10. brontosaurus dinosaur The the was largest plant-eating

    ____

ALIKE AND DIFFERENT

Directions: When you tell how things are alike, you are comparing them. When you tell how they are different, you are contrasting them. Tell how each pair listed below is alike and how it is different.

1. ABSOLUTE DATING — RELATIVE DATING
   a. How they are alike:
   ____
   b. How they are different:
   ____

2. MOLD — CAST
   a. How they are alike:
   ____
   b. How they are different:
   ____

3. PETRIFICATION — PRESERVATION
   a. How they are alike:
   ____
   b. How they are different:
   ____

4. SUPERPOSITION — CROSSCUTTING
   a. How they are alike:
   ____
   b. How they are different:
   ____

5. MESOZOIC ERA — CENOZOIC ERA
   a. How they are alike:
   ____
   b. How they are different:
   ____

RELATIVE DATING

Directions: Suppose you have been asked to explain to a class the principles of crosscutting and superposition. Use the diagrams below as a guide. Write the script of your lecture on the lines below.

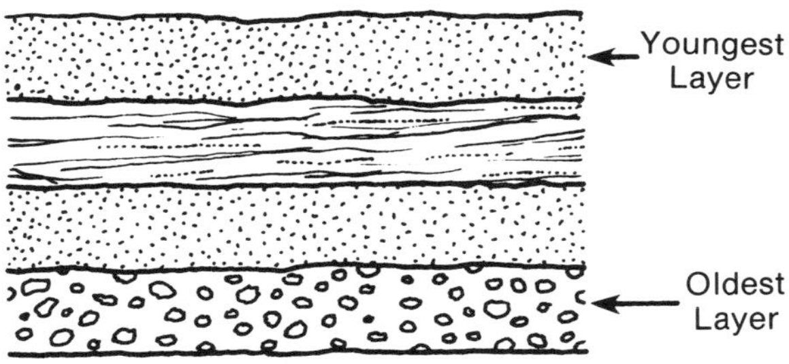

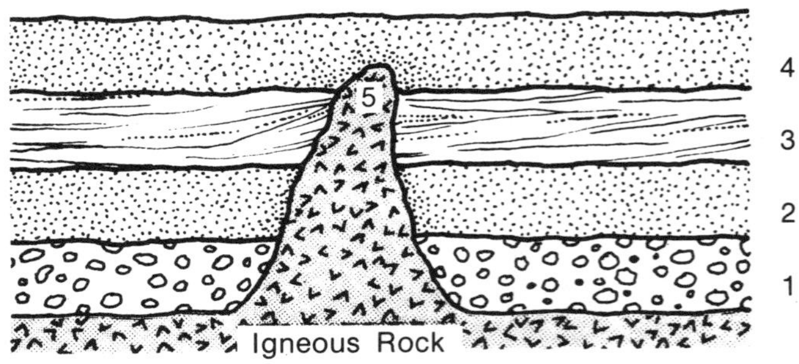

CLASSIFICATION

Directions: Read the words and terms in each category below. Choose the two items in each group that do not belong. Cross them out. Write them in their correct categories. Then add two new words of your own to each category.

Earth and Moon

tides
dunes
terrestrial
paleontologist
crater
season

____
____
____
____

Weathering

anemometer
chemical
mesa
freezing and cracking
dissolving
forming soil

____
____
____
____

Earth's History

geologic time
mechanical
Devonian
era
spiral
crosscutting

____
____
____
____

Weather Report

temperature
maria
relative humidity
meteorologist
fronts
hurricane
lunar

____
____
____
____

Land Forms

rust
gullies
cirques
moraine
delta
talus
Milky Way

____
____
____
____

Stars and Galaxies

dwarf
Precambrian
blue-white
magnitude
isobars
constellation
supernova

____
____
____
____

"-OLOGIST" CAREERS CROSSWORD PUZZLE

Directions: The suffix **-ology** means "the study of." When -ist is added, the two together, -ologist, means "a person who studies..." The crossword puzzle below contains the names of "people who study" particular topics in earth science. The names are listed below. Use a dictionary to look up any terms that you do not know.

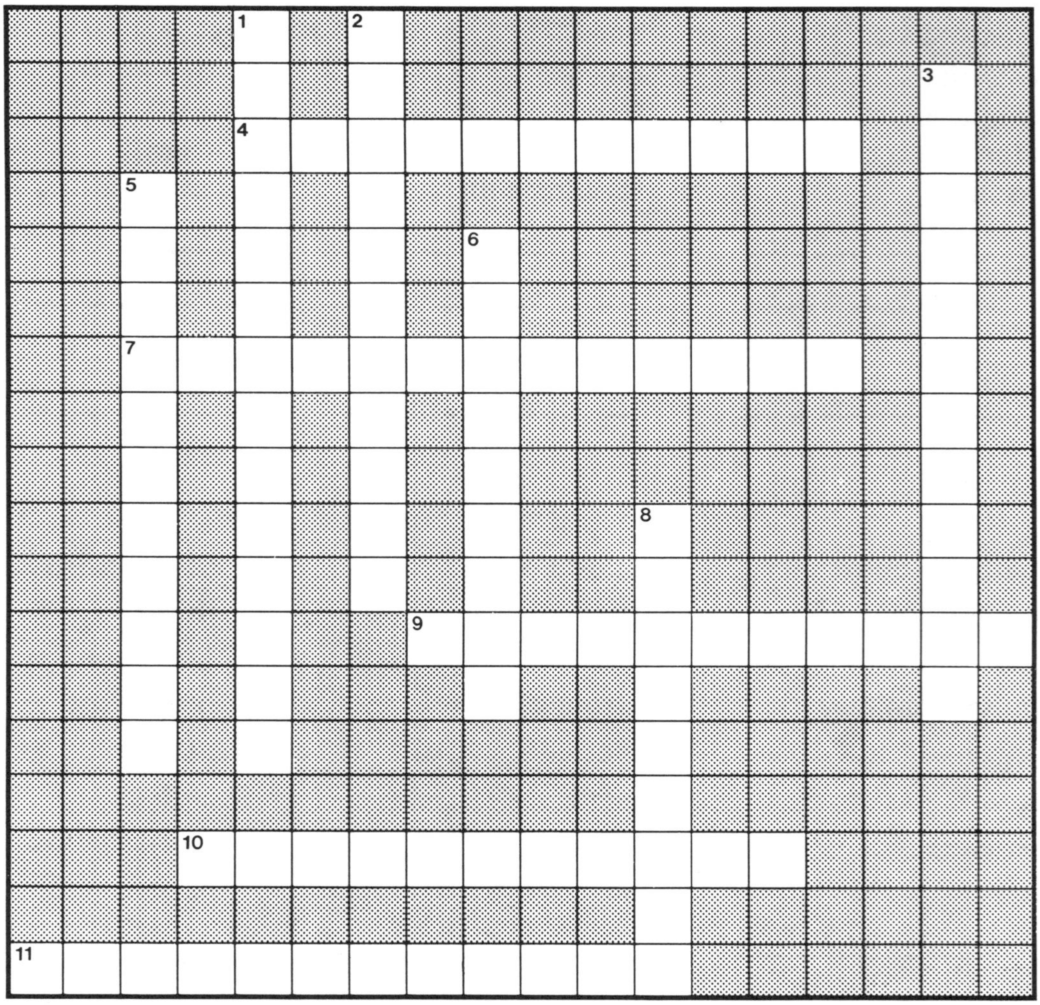

Across

4. Studies rocks
7. Studies weather
9. Studies stars
10. Studies water
11. Studies minerals

Down

1. Studies fossils
2. Studies oil deposits
3. Studies caves
5. Studies the universe, or cosmos
6. Studies animal life
8. Studies earth forms

Paleontologist	Lithologist
Cosmologist	Zoologist
Hydrologist	Speleologist
Geologist	Astrologist
Meteorologist	Petrologist
Minerologist	

Which person is not a scientist?

THE MOST IMPORTANT THING ABOUT . . .

(This research writing activity may be done individually or in groups.)

Directions: Choose one area of earth science from the box.

Earth's Water	Weathering and Erosion	Weather and Climate
Earth's History	Forces in the Earth	Earth's Atmosphere
Rocks		

List as many topics as you can think of about the area you selected. Use your textbook as a reference. For example, if you chose "Earth's Water," the topics could be: precipitation, fresh water, salt water, water cycle, streams and rivers, lakes and ponds, clouds, oceans, and so forth. Record your area and topics in the following spaces.

My Area Is: ________________________________

Possible Topics: ________________________________

____

____

____

____

____

Look at your list of possible topics and choose the one that you feel is the most interesting. Record the topic you chose.

My Topic Is: ________________________________

Use your textbook. Write down all the significant details you can find about the topic you chose. You may also use any other references that you find. After writing the details down, number them in order of decreasing importance. For example, if you had chosen "Clouds" as your topic, you could write down the following:

Importance	**Details**
2	Clouds are collections of water droplets.
1	Clouds bring rain.
5	Clouds hold in the heat of the earth.
3	The darker the cloud, the more water it contains.
4	The biggest, darkest rain clouds are called cumulonimbus.
6	On a hot summer day, clouds provide a shaded break.

THE MOST IMPORTANT THING ABOUT . . . (Part 2)

Record your topics and their importance in the spaces provided.

Importance	Details
______________________	____
______________________	____
______________________	____
______________________	____
______________________	____
______________________	____
______________________	____
______________________	____

Now, write your significant details in the form shown below. You will emphasize the most important thing on your list by writing it in this form.

> The most important thing about clouds is that they bring rain.
>
> Clouds are collections of water droplets.
> The darker the cloud, the more water it contains.
> The biggest, darkest rain clouds are called cumulonimbus.
> Clouds hold in the heat of the earth.
> On a hot summer day, clouds provide a shaded break.
>
> But, the most important thing about clouds is that they bring rain.

The most important thing about ____

____

____

____

____

____

____

But, the most important thing about ____________________________________

____

____

THE MOST IMPORTANT THING ABOUT . . . (Part 3)

Now, rewrite each of your statements to say the same thing in another way. The example using clouds is rewritten here to demonstrate.

> The most important thing about clouds is that the rain falls from them.
> Drops of water collect in clouds.
> Darker clouds carry more water than lighter ones.
> Cumulonimbus clouds, the darkest clouds, usually bring rain.
> Clouds hold in the earth's heat.
> Clouds can block the sun on hot summer days.
> But, the most important thing about clouds is that the rain falls from them.

Write your sample here:

The most important thing about ________________________________

____

____

____

____

____

____

But, the most important thing about ________________________________

____

____

You are now ready to write your final statement on the topic you chose. Compare your two versions of the most important thing. Choose the best statement for each idea. Write your final version neatly on page 64. The final version for the example is shown below.

> The most important thing about clouds is that they bring rain.
> Drops of water collect in clouds.
> The darker the cloud, the more water it contains.
> The biggest, darkest rain clouds are called cumulonimbus clouds.
> Clouds hold in the earth's heat.
> On a hot summer day, clouds provide a shaded break.
> But, the most important thing about clouds is that they bring rain.

The most important thing about . . .

The most important thing about ____________________

____

____

____

____

____

____

____

____

____

____

But, the most important thing about ____________________

____

____

____

____

Author(s): ____________________

____